To My dear ~~Daughter~~

B~~etty~~

1985

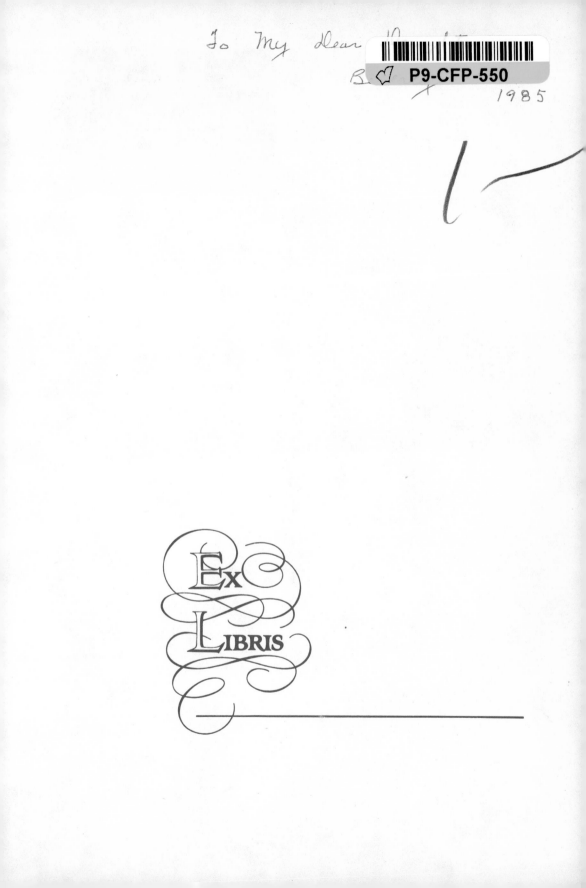

Ex
Libris

The Priceless Gift

The Poems of
Helen Steiner Rice

The *Priceless Gift*

A Fond Recollection
by Fred Bauer

Guideposts
CARMEL · NEW YORK 10512

ACKNOWLEDGEMENTS

Poems of Helen Steiner Rice are used with permission of the Helen Steiner Rice
Foundation, c/o Strauss, Troy and Ruehlmann Co., L.P.A., 2100 Central Trust
Center, Cincinnati, Ohio 45202.
"The Ballad of Befana" Copyright © 1957 by Phyllis McGinley.
Reprinted by permission of Curtis Brown, Ltd.
Guideposts Associates, Inc., Carmel, N.Y. 10512. The author expresses
grateful appreciation for permission to reprint in these pages works of his
which originally appeared in the following publications: "It Was That Night"
from Guideposts magazine copyright © 1964; "The Faded Blue Blanket" from
Guideposts Christmas Greeting, copyright © 1964; "Child-Light" from
Guideposts Christmas Greeting, copyright © 1972; "So Gentle" from
Guideposts Christmas Greeting, copyright © 1976; "Time for Christmas"
from The Guideposts Christmas Treasury copyright © 1972.
Unless otherwise noted, Scripture quotations in this book are from the King
James Version of the Bible.
Design by Holly Johnson at the Angelica Design Group, Ltd.
Illustrations by Judith Fast

Library of Congress Cataloging in Publication Data

Rice, Helen Steiner
    The priceless gift.

        1. Christian poetry, American   I. Bauer, Fred, fl. 1968-
II. Title.
PS 3568.I28P77 1984   811.54   84-15417
ISBN 0-89952-060-X

**This Guideposts edition is published by special arrangement with
Littlebrook Publishing Inc.**

Time is not measured
   by the years that we live,
But by the deeds that we do
   and the joys that we give.
            —*Helen Steiner Rice*

Contents

Introduction

While working with Helen Steiner Rice on her autobiography, *In the Vineyard of the Lord*, and later when we were laying plans for her *Poems of Faith* and this book, I repeated the prediction that her verses would still be quoted "a hundred years from now."

She modestly demurred, saying that "others more talented than I will take up the torch, and no one will remember my humble efforts."

That conversation came back to me while I was organizing this book. It has been three years now since her death and the question as to the lasting quality of her poems can be raised. Death often marks the end of significant interest in creative talents, be they writers, artists, musicians. What about interest in Mrs. Rice's rhyming messages of faith? Has her popularity, far and away the most impressive of any inspirational poet of this century, showed any sign of waning?

Though it is obviously too early to make any long term assumptions, it can be said with certainty that to date there is still immense admiration for her poems and that their popularity, if anything, is even greater than when she was alive. Her books and greeting cards continue to inspire millions.

People write me frequently to share how they or a family member or a friend were encouraged by something Mrs. Rice had written. Often they want to know more about the woman and her faith. It is a natural inquisitiveness, even though Mrs. Rice was forever trying to deflect personal interest in herself.

"What I am is contained in my poems," she told me again and again. "There's nothing more to tell."

Of course there was and there is, and filling in some of the details about this dedicated Christian poet is in part the purpose of this book. But *The Priceless Gift* is not just a book about a very unique woman of faith. She would have been embarrassed by such a narrowly focused spotlight.

Rather it is a book that draws from her life and her writings, and the work of others who shared her faith in Christ, truths about the rewards of giving that are not only timeless, but priceless. My hope in sharing some very personal memories is that you will come to appreciate her dedication and commitment as much as I do.

Perhaps the best way to clarify my intention is to begin by quoting some special lines Mrs. Rice often used to preface her books...

> Show me the way not to fortune or fame,
> Not how to win laurels or praise for my name—
> But show me the way to spread the Great Story
> That "Thine is the Kingdom and Power and Glory."

Fred Bauer
Princeton, New Jersey

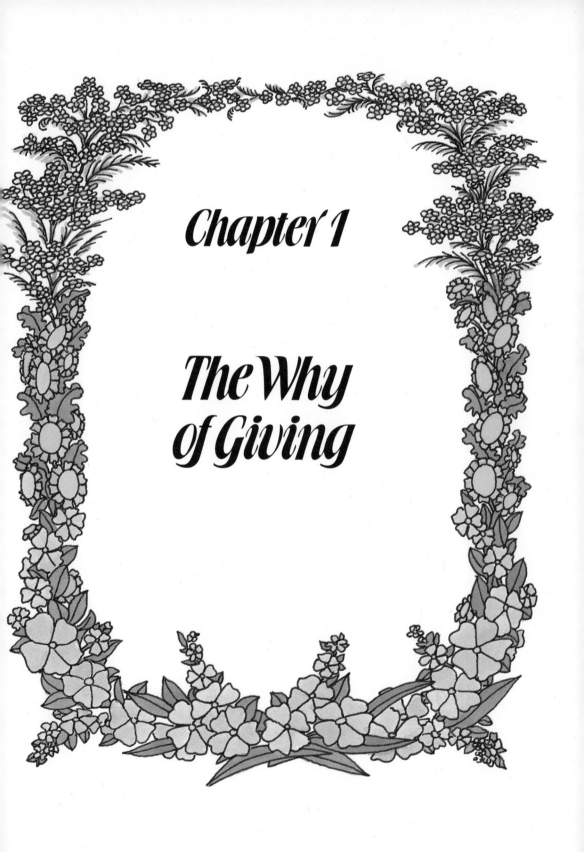

Chapter 1

The Why of Giving

The Priceless Gift

Now Christmas is a season
     for joy and merrymaking,
A time for gifts and presents
     for giving and for taking,
A festive, friendly, happy time
     when everyone is gay—
But have we really felt
     the greatness of the day?
For through the centuries the world
     has wandered far away
From the beauty and the meaning
     of the Holy Christmas Day.
For Christmas is a heavenly gift
     that only God can give,
It's ours just for the asking
     for as long as we shall live,
It can't be bought or bartered,
     it can't be won or sold,
It doesn't cost a penny
     and it's worth far more than gold.
It isn't bright and gleaming
     for eager eyes to see,
It can't be wrapped in tinsel
     or placed beneath a tree,
It isn't soft and shimmering
     for reaching hands to touch,
Or some expensive luxury
     you've wanted very much.

15

For the Priceless Gift of Christmas
    is meant just for the heart,
And we receive it only
    when we become a part
Of the Kingdom and the Glory
    which is ours to freely take,
For God sent the Holy Christ Child
    at Christmas for our sake
So man might come to Know Him
    and feel His Presence near,
And see the many miracles
    performed while He was here.
And this Priceless Gift of Christmas
    is within the reach of all,
The rich, the poor, the young and old,
    the greatest and the small.
So take His Priceless Gift of Love,
    reach out and you'll receive,
And the only payment that God asks
    is just that you Believe.

hite feathers.

That's what the skyful of snowflakes resembled as they swirled, dipsy-doodle to earth that December night in Cincinnati. And as the whiteness accumulated, the city was transformed into a winter wonderland.

Street lights took bites out of the darkness and formed shimmering cylinders while the snow-muted Christmas decorations from storefronts below and apartments above created miniature rainbows of beauty.

Cold as it was I don't remember feeling chilled as I made my way crosstown. I had come to Cincinnati to spend a few days interviewing Helen Steiner Rice for a book on which we were collaborating.

After working the day with her at her office, I had offered to take her out for dinner, but she said she was not up to it. (In her mid-seventies, Mrs. Rice's health was a troubling matter and, though she tried not to complain, it was obviously frustrating for her to have a body that sometimes refused to cooperate with her fertile mind and robust spirit.)

"If you won't let me take you out for dinner, I'll bring dinner to you," I announced.

"That would be nice," she brightened. When I asked what she would like to eat, she told me that her appetite wasn't very good, but "if you could find some good Chinese food…" A

17

postscript to her acceptance was that she had some scrapbooks at her apartment that would add to my research.

So about 7 o'clock, I left my hotel, picked up two Chinese dinners at a recommended restaurant and set out through the snow to Mrs. Rice's apartment a few blocks away. When I arrived, white and wet, she made a motherly fuss and went to put on hot tea while I opened the dinners, which we ate at the kitchen table.

Mrs. Rice was in rare form that night as she animatedly recalled incidents from her eventful life. Sometimes I found it difficult to keep up, because she not only spoke in 300-words-a-minute bursts, but she had the agility of a quarterhorse when it came to changing directions. One minute she would be talking about something from her childhood and then segue into another subject, something that happened 30 years later, with little or no signal. She reminded me of my elementary math teacher, Miss Hoskinson, a woman who, like Mrs. Rice, had a flamboyant personality and a quick-draw mind that required total concentration if one were to gain full measure from her pronouncements.

Most of the evening we sat at her desk where she sorted through materials that she had gathered over many years: pictures, newspaper and magazine clippings, notes, letters, greeting cards bearing her rhymes as well as new-to-me verses that she had written to friends on special occasions.

While she passed things to me, I kept a tape recorder running to ensure what I didn't get down on paper would not be lost. Sometimes I'd interrupt and ask her to elaborate.

"Is that a copy of the card that fell into the hands of the

Lawrence Welk people?" When she said that it was, I asked her to retell me the story, which she did.

Up until December of 1960, relatively few people outside the greeting card field knew the name Helen Steiner Rice. Though she had written verses for cards for nearly 30 of her 60 years, she, like many other poets in the business, labored in obscurity. But that all changed for Mrs. Rice when an entertainer by the name of Alladin recited her poem, "The Priceless Gift of Christmas," on the Lawrence Welk Show before a national TV audience. Alladin had received the card from his sister, who had been impressed with it and she called it to her performing brother's attention.

He likewise thought it commendable, so he brought it to rehearsal with him and suggested that it might be right for their upcoming Christmas show. Welk agreed and that is how Alladin came to share it with millions of Americans.

Because the name of the poet was not on the card, the author received no credit when Alladin read it, and in most cases that would have been the end of the story. But the response to the poem was unprecedented. Literally thousands of viewers wrote for copies and to inquire about the poem's author.

In one fell swoop, Helen Steiner Rice received more attention than she had in decades of writing for Gibson Greeting Cards. What followed was better than 20 years of unstinting adulation for her poems of inspiration. In addition to greeting cards, which sold in the millions, collections of her poems were gathered into books that became bestsellers. Her verses were used on radio and television, set to music, reprinted in magazines and recited by speakers the world over. Plaques, vases, samplers and the like bearing her words were hard for store owners to keep in stock.

But no one was more surprised—or more unaffected—than Mrs. Rice.

"What would have happened to Helen Steiner Rice if she had not been 'discovered' on the Welk program?" I asked.

"I would have gone right on writing just the same," she replied. "You see, before I began writing, I used to speak a lot and I never let the size of the audience determine the quality of my effort. I always was taught that anything worth doing is worth doing right."

(Later, the subject came up again and she opined that her success was "ordained by God." Adding, "Nothing of significance happens to us that isn't part of His grand design.")

"But why do you think He picked you?" I pressed.

"Maybe because I have such an uncomplicated faith," she answered with a smile. "I have no doubts about God or about His love for me. He gave His Son; I gave Him my life. And because I write, I gave that to Him, too, and He has taken my simple gift and multiplied it a million times. He can accomplish miraculous things when we give ourselves to Him completely, without reservations or qualifications."

That night, walking back to my hotel through the snow, and many times since, I've thought about that statement and how much spiritual wisdom and truth it contains.

What Christmas Means to Me

Christmas to me is a gift from above—
     a gift of salvation born of God's love.
For far beyond what my mind comprehends
     my eternal future completely depends.
On that first Christmas night centuries ago,
     when God sent His Son to the earth below,
For if the Christ Child had not been born
     there would be no rejoicing on Easter morn.
For only because Christ was born and died,
     and hung on a cross to be crucified,
Can worldly sinners like you and me,
     be fit to live in eternity. . . .
So Christmas is more than getting and giving,
     it's the why and the wherefore of infinite living,
It's the positive proof for doubting God never,
     for in His Kingdom life is forever.
And that is the reason that on Christmas Day,
     I can only kneel down and prayerfully say,
"Thank You, God, for sending Your Son,
     so when my work on earth is done,
I can look at last on Your holy face,
     knowing You save me alone by Your grace.

For many years—in the '30s, '40s and '50s—Mrs. Rice wrote poems like *What Christmas Means to Me* and sent them to her friends as her personal greeting. Most "first-class" greeting card companies considered religious sentiments inappropriate for their lines, she told me. But once the public learned about her bent for "faith poems," she was asked to search her files for others.

Though she stated it often in different ways, the essence of her Christmas message is captured in the lines, "Christmas is more than getting and giving, it's the why and the wherefore of infinite living..."

Her inspirational efforts placed her in the select company of gifted writers who for time immemorial have tried to explain the "why" of giving—God's and ours. Invariably, the giving focuses on Christmas, because everything about that event pertains to giving.

What was man's response to the gift of God's Son? St. Luke tells us about the immediate celebration—a heavenly chorus praising the Christ Child and adoring shepherds who came to worship Him. But St. Matthew tells about the Wise Men, and that is the basis for our gift-giving at Christmastime:

"And, lo, the star, which they saw in the east, went before them, till it came and stood over where the young child was. When they saw the star, they rejoiced with exceeding great joy. And when they were come into the house, they saw the young child with Mary his mother, and fell down and worshipped him; and when they had opened their treasures, they presented unto him gifts; gold and frankincense and myrrh..." *(Matthew 2:9-11)*

22   The Wise Men, although often referred to as kings were,

according to scholars, more likely astrologers. In truth, there are only two kings in the story, Herod, and the King of Kings.

The story of the Wise Men and their quest has fueled the imagination of many writers throughout the centuries as they speculated about what prompted those seekers to set out, how they chose the gifts that they did, how long it took them to reach Bethlehem and the problems they encountered along the way.

One of Mrs. Rice's favorite stories was set to rhyme by the late Phyllis McGinley, who must have asked herself why there were no "wise" women in the entourage.

The Ballad of Befana

Befana the housewife scrubbing her pane,
Saw three old sages ride down the lane,
Saw three gray travelers pass her door—
Gaspar, Balthazar, Melchior.
"Where journey you, sirs?" she asked of them.
Balthazar answered, "To Bethlehem,
For we have news of a marvelous thing.
Born in a stable is Christ the King."
"Give him my welcome!"
Then Gaspar smiled,
"Come with us, mistress, to greet the Child."
"Oh, happily, happily would I fare,
Were my dusting through and I'd polished the stair."
Old Melchior leaned on his saddle horn.
"Then send but a gift to the small Newborn."

23

"Oh, gladly, gladly I'd send Him one,
Were the hearthstone swept and my weaving done.
As soon as ever I've baked my bread,
I'll fetch Him a pillow for His head,
And a coverlet too," Befana said.
"When the rooms are aired and the linen dry,
I'll look for the Babe."
But the three rode by.
She worked for a day and a night and a day,
Then, gifts in her hands, took up her way.
But she never could find where the Christ Child lay.
And still she wanders at Christmastide,
Houseless, whose house was all her pride,
Whose heart was tardy, whose gifts were late;
Wanders and knocks at every gate,
Crying, "Good people, the bells begin!
Put off your toiling and let love in."

—*PM*

24

Mrs. Rice echoed a similar lament in one of her most insightful verses.

Meeting Angels Unaware

On life's busy thoroughfare,
We meet with angels unaware,
But we are too busy to see or hear,
Too busy to sense that God is near,
Too busy to stop and recognize
The grief that lies in another's eyes,
Too busy to offer to help or share,
Too busy to sympathize or care,
Too busy to do the good things we should,
Telling ourselves we would if we could.
But life is too swift and the pace is too great
And we dare not pause for we might be late
For our next appointment which means so much,
We are willing to brush off the Saviour's touch,
And we tell ourselves there will come a day,
We will have more time to pause on our way,
But before we know it life's sun has set,
And we've passed the Saviour, but never met,
For hurrying along life's thoroughfare,
We passed Him by and remained unaware
That within the very sight of our eye,
Unnoticed, the Son of God passed by.

And I, too, have pondered the "why" of giving. In a little story for *Guideposts* I considered the shepherds' "why":

The Faded Blue Blanket

...The most frightened shepherd that night was little Ladius, just ten. He cowered behind his three older brothers when the blinding star lit the hillside. When the angel appeared, he hid behind a huge rock.

Yet after Ladius heard the glad news, fear left him and he limped back to his brothers who were planning to set out for Bethlehem.

"Who will tend the sheep?" asked Samuel, the oldest at sixteen. Ladius, leaning against his shepherd's crook to support a foot crippled from birth, volunteered.

"I'd only slow you down. Let me stay with the sheep." He bit his lower lip as he talked. The brothers protested weakly, then made plans to go.

"We must each take a gift," said Samuel. One brother chose his flint to start a fire for the Christ Child. Another picked meadow lilies to make a garland for the King. Samuel decided on his most precious possession, his golden ring.

"Here, take my blanket to Him," said Ladius. It was badly worn—a faded blue with patches.

"No, Ladius," said Samuel tenderly. "The blanket is too tattered to give even a beggar—let alone a King. Besides, you will need it to stay warm tonight."

The brothers departed, leaving Ladius alone by the fire. He laid his head on the blanket and buried his face in his hands. Tears forced their way between his fingers, but soon sleep soothed the boy's heartbreak. *The world in silent stillness lay...*

"Are you coming, Ladius?" called a voice. Standing nearby was the same angel who had brought the news. "You wanted to see the Child, didn't you?"

"Yes," Ladius said, nodding, "but I must stay here."

"My name is Gabriel," said the angel. "Your sheep will be watched. Take my hand—and bring your blanket. The Child will need it."

Suddenly, Ladius was outside a stable. Kneeling by a manger were his brothers. He wanted to call out, but the angel lifted a finger to his lips.

"Give me the blanket," Gabriel whispered. The angel took it and quietly covered the Baby. But the blanket was no longer faded. Now it glistened like the brilliance of a new day. Returning, Gabriel squeezed Ladius' hand. "Your gift was best because you gave all you had..."

"Wake up, Ladius, wake up." The boy rubbed his eyes and tried to shield them from the glaring sun. Hovering over him was Samuel and the others.

"Did you find Him?" asked Ladius.

"Yes, we did," answered Samuel. "We saw the Christ Child, and I'll tell you about it, but first explain why you were sleeping without your blanket."

Ladius looked all about wonderingly. His faded blue blanket was nowhere to be found—then or thereafter.

—*FB*

Poet Christiana Rossetti put herself in the Holy Night tableau and tried to imagine what she might have given in response to God's gift of His only Son. She articulated it this way...

In the Bleak Midwinter

...Our God, heaven cannot hold Him,
Nor earth sustain;
Heaven and earth shall flee away,
When He comes to reign;
In the bleak midwinter
A stable place sufficed
The Lord Almighty,
Jesus Christ.

Angels and archangels
May have gathered there,
Cherubim and seraphim

Thronged the air;
But His mother only,
In her maiden bliss
Worshipped the Beloved
With a kiss.

What can I give Him,
Poor as I am?
If I were a shepherd,
I would bring a lamb;
If I were a wise man,
I would do my part;
Yet what can I give Him—
Give Him my heart.

—*CR*

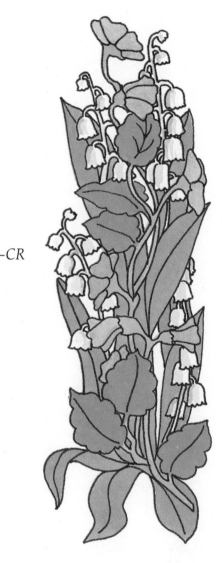

The answer to the question, "Why do we give?" may lie in the fact that people who love life deeply, live it fully and appreciate it sincerely feel compelled to offer something in return for the blessings that have come their way. As the beloved hymn writer Isaac Watts said so beautifully, "Love so amazing, so divine, demands my life, my soul, my all."

How sad when some people think they have achieved their station in life by themselves and without help. In addition to spiritual blindness, they suffer from an acute case of ungratefulness. There are no self-made men or women in life. We all have many to whom we owe great debts. And the starting place for our thanksgiving is God Himself, whose Son observed, "It is more blessed to give than to receive." *(Acts 20:35)*

Mrs. Rice knew the satisfaction that comes to those who are generous with the bounty God has so lavishly showered upon them:

Flowers Leave Their Fragrance on the Hand of the Giver

There's an old Chinese proverb
    that if practiced each day,
Would change the whole world
    in a wonderful way—
Its truth is so simple,
    it's so easy to do,
And it works every time
    and successfully, too.
For you can't do a kindness
    without a reward,
Not in silver or gold
    but in joy from the Lord—
You can't light a candle
    to show others the way
Without feeling the warmth
    of that bright little ray.
And you can't pluck a rose,
    all fragrant with dew,
Without part of its fragrance
    remaining with you.

Life's True Yardstick

Don't count your age
    by the years you've known,
But by the friends you have made
    and the kindnesses sown,
For life is not measured
    by the years that you live,
But by the deeds you do
    and the joys you give.

Everybody Everywhere
Needs Somebody Sometime

Everybody, everywhere, no matter
    what his station,
Has moments of deep loneliness
    and quiet desperation,
For this lost and lonely feeling
    is inherent in mankind,
It is just the Spirit speaking
    as God tries again to find
An opening in the "worldly wall"
    man builds against God's touch,
For he feels so self-sufficient
    that he does not need God much,
So he vainly goes on struggling
    to find some explanation,
For these disturbing, lonely moods
    of inner isolation,
But the answer keeps eluding him
    for in his finite mind,
He does not even recognize
    that he can never find
The reason for life's emptiness
    unless he learns to share
The problems and the burdens
    that surround him everywhere.
But when his eyes are opened
    and he looks with love at others,

He begins to see not strangers,
    but understanding brothers.
So open up your hardened hearts
    and let God enter in,
He only wants to help you
    a new life to begin,
And every day's a good day
    to lose yourself to others,
And any time a good time
    to see mankind as brothers,
And this can only happen
    when you realize it's true,
That everyone needs someone
    and that someone is you.

Heart Gifts

It's not the things that can be bought
    that are life's richest treasure,
It's just the little "heart gifts"
    that money cannot measure...
A cheerful smile, a friendly word,
    a sympathetic nod,
Are priceless little treasures
    from the storehouse of our God...
They are the things that cannot be bought
    with silver or with gold,
For thoughtfulness and kindness
    and love are never sold...
They are the priceless things in life
    for which no one can pay,
And the giver finds rich recompense
    in GIVING THEM AWAY.

Chapter 2

The When of Giving

For God So Loved the World

Our Father up in Heaven
    long, long years ago,
Looked down in His great mercy
    upon the earth below,
And saw that folks were lonely
    and lost in deep despair,
And so he said, "I'll send My Son
    to walk among them there,
So they can hear Him speaking
    and feel His nearness, too,
And see the many miracles
    that Faith alone can do,
For if man really sees Him
    and can touch His healing hand,
I know it will be easier
    to believe and understand."
And so The Holy Christ Child
    came down to live on earth,
And that is why we celebrate
    His holy, wondrous birth,
And that is why at Christmas
    the world becomes aware
That heaven may seem far away,
    but God is everywhere.

A story dear to Helen Steiner Rice's heart was about a man named Harold who, one winter night, faced a dilemma. Kind-hearted and sensitive, he took particular concern for life's "little" people and little creatures. So it was not out of character that he grew anxious when he looked out the window of his den one sub-zero evening and in the shadows saw some birds huddling in the snow-covered bushes, trying desperately to keep from freezing.

"They're helpless," he told his wife as he put on his coat and headed outside. His plan was to open the garage doors and spread some seed on the floor in hope that the birds would take refuge there.

But it failed to work. When he returned a while later, the grain was untouched. Not a single bird had accepted his hospitality. They're afraid, he thought. How can I show them I want to help? How can I tell them I'm trying to save them?

Then, he got an inspiration: He would leave a light burning. Maybe it would allay their fears. So he turned on the garage light, and when he checked a while later there where dozens of birds inside, dozens who had taken refuge from the cold.

Later, when he told a friend the story, the man smiled. "You know, Harold, God once had a similar problem. He wanted to tell His creation, men and women, that He wasn't a God of

41

wrath, but a God of Love, personally caring and concerned about them. But they feared Him, and He had trouble making them understand.

"His solution was to send a messenger from Heaven to demonstrate His love. So God sent His only Son, Jesus, to preach and teach and love and heal and redeem. And they called Him the Light of the World."

I Am the Light of the World

Oh, Father, up in heaven
    we have wandered far away
From the Holy little Christ Child
    who was born on Christmas Day,
And the promise of salvation
    that God promised when Christ died.
We have often vaguely questioned,
    even doubted and denied,
We've forgotten why God sent us
    Jesus Christ, His only Son,
And in arrogance and ignorance,
    it's our will, not Thine be done.
Oh, forgive us our transgressions,
    and stir our souls within,
And make us conscious
    that there is no joy in sin,
And shed Thy Light upon us
    as Christmas comes again,
So we may strive for peace on earth,
    and good will among men.

And God, in Thy great wisdom,
Thy mercy and Thy love,
Endow us with the virtue
that we have so little of.

Why did God choose to give His Son to Earth at the time that he did? The only answer is that in God's sight, the time was ripe. The prophets of the Old Testament had foretold the coming of a Messiah. Daniel *(9:24-27)* suggested a schedule, which indicated the time was at hand. And Isaiah *(7:14)* wrote, "Behold, a virgin shall conceive, and bear a son, and shall call His name Immanuel" (which means *God with us*). He was to be born out of the lineage of David in the small village of Bethlehem ("Though thou be little among the thousands [of villages] of Judah, yet out of thee shall He come forth unto me that is to be ruler in Israel." *(Micah 5:2)*.

Under the generalship of Pompey, Palestine had fallen to the Romans in 63 B.C. The harsh and paranoid Herod had succeeded his father to the throne and had proceeded to inflict his cruel punishment upon the Jews. No people could have been more in need of a Saviour.

So all was in readiness for God's plan, and the Word became flesh. God moved from the shadowy wings of human history to earth's fully lighted center stage. The immediate drama began with Zacharias and his childless wife Elisabeth. First, this aging couple learned they were to become parents of a son (John, the Baptist), the Evangel who would go before Christ with the power of Elias and "make ready a people prepared for the Lord." *(Luke 1:17)*. Then, Elisabeth's cousin, Mary, visited her and shared even more astounding news. Following Elisabeth's famous salutation, "Blessed art thou among women, and blessed is the fruit of thy womb," Mary delivered one of the most beautiful poems in the Bible, what is commonly known as "The Magnificat." *(Luke 1:46-55)*

My soul doth magnify the Lord,
And my spirit hath rejoiced
    in God my Saviour.
For He hath regarded the low estate
    of His handmaiden: for, behold,
    from henceforth all generations
    shall call me blessed.
For He that is mighty hath done
    to me great things;
    and holy is His name.
And His mercy is on them that fear
    Him from generation to generation.
He hath shewed strength with His arm;
    He hath scattered the proud in
    the imagination of their hearts.
He hath put down the mighty
    from their seats, and exalted
    them of low degree.
He hath filled the hungry with
    good things; and the rich
    He hath sent empty away.

He hath holpen His servant Israel,
in remembrance of His mercy;
As He spake to our fathers,
to Abraham, and to His seed for ever.

Then came the Event of the ages. The Bible tells it in a few words, but they have inspired millions of poets to describe when the Babe of Bethlehem arrived, including this gem by Mrs. Rice.

Unto Us a Child is Born

God sent the little Christ Child
So man might understand
That a little child shall lead them
To that unknown Promised Land.
For God in His great wisdom
Knew that men would rise to power,
And forget His holy precepts
In their great triumphal hour.
He knew that they would question,
And doubt the Holy Birth,
And turn their time and talents
To the pleasures of this earth.
But every new discovery
Is an open avenue
To more and greater mysteries—
Man's search is never through.
For man can never fathom

45

The mysteries of the Lord,
Or understand His promise
Of a heavenly reward.
For no one but a little Child
With simple faith and love
Can lead man's straying footsteps
To higher realms above.

The story is told of a homesick college freshman who was too far away to join his family for Christmas. Attempting to cheer him up, a school official asked what the student would most like for Christmas. Turning to a picture of his father on the bureau, the young man said, "I'd like him to step out of that frame."

A search of my Christmas files produced these attempts of mine to address that historical moment when God "stepped out of the frame" and became flesh. Most of the following were published on greeting cards:

It Was That Night

It was that ethereal night when
  a matchless star stood glowing in the East,
  trailing a man, a woman, a burdened beast,

It was that incredible night when
  an innkeeper became the first to say,
  "I have no room for You today."

It was that incomparable night when
  Gabriel came ecstatic to earth,
  proclaiming glad tidings of a royal birth,

It was that immortal night when
     a caring God reached gently down to lay,
     His supreme gift, Love, upon the hay.

—FB

So Gentle

So gentle, soft and crying,
He hardly looked the part
Of one sent by God almighty
To change the human heart.

—FB

Child-Light

They were hoping for a king,
A man of wealth and might,
But God sent forth a babe,
A child to shed His light.

—FB

His Gift Was Love

His gift was Love,
His mission, Release,
His promise, Life,
His legacy, Peace.

—FB

47

Time for Christmas

Christmas is a time of anticipation,
When hope becomes a shining star,
When children's wishes become prayers,
And days are X'ed on calendar.

Christmas is a time for healing,
When disagreers and disagreements meet,
When long-time wounds are mended,
And love drives hatred to retreat.

Christmas is a time for patience,
When we try anew to mold
Our lives in the image of Him,
Whose birthday we uphold.

Christmas is a time for giving,
The Wise Men brought their best,
But Christ showed that self gifts,
Out-give all the rest.

Christmas is a time for understanding
People and customs throughout the world,
When for all too brief a season
The banner of peace is unfurled.

Christmas is a time for children
No matter what their age,
Spirit is the only ticket,
And heart the only gauge.

Christmas is a time for learning,
A time new truths unfold,
When not-so-innocent children
Often teach the old.

Christmas is a time for sharing,
A time for needy hands to clasp,
A time for stretching out in faith
With a reach that exceeds our grasp.

Christmas is a time for love,
A time for inhibitions to shed,
A time for showing that we care,
A time for words too long unsaid.

Christmas is a time to remember
Timeless stories from days of yore,
A time to ponder what's ahead,
A time to open another door.

—FB

The subject of God's timing is an endless puzzlement for humankind. Probably all of us have at one time or another grown impatient with our condition or circumstance and have questioned our heavenly Father's timetable. When needs press in on us and we petition Him for directions, answers or relief, we expect Him to give our concerns immediate attention. But, alas, we wait. We receive no clear-cut guidance. We stew. We fret. We fidget. We complain.

Being told that God's timing is always right—never too early, never too late—is of little solace. "This is not something that can wait," we respond. "Can't God see I'm hurting? Doesn't He understand? Where is His mercy?"

Mrs. Rice spoke to those questions about God's timing with these reassuring words:

The Seasons of the Soul

Why am I cast down
    and despondently sad
When I long to be happy
    and joyous and glad?
Why is my heart heavy
    with unfathomable weight
As I try to escape
    this soul-saddened state?
I ask myself often
    what makes life this way?

Why is the song silenced
     in a heart that was gay?
And then with God's help
     it all becomes clear.
The soul has its seasons
     just the same as the year.
I too must pass through
     life's autumn of dying,
A desolate period
     a heart hurt and crying,
Followed by winter
     in whose frostbitten hand
My heart is as frozen
     as the snow-covered land.
Yes, man too must pass
     through the seasons God sends
Content in the knowledge
     that everything ends.
And, oh, what a blessing
     to know there are reasons
And to find that our soul
     must, too, have its seasons—
Bounteous seasons,
     and barren ones, too,
Times for rejoicing
     and times to be blue,
But meeting these seasons
     of dark desolation

With strength that is born
    of anticipation
That comes from knowing
    that "Autumn-time Sadness"
Will surely be followed
    by a "Springtime of Gladness."

Once we learn with heart and head that God has a design for our lives, we can understand the Bible verse that advises, "...all things work together for good to them that love God, to them who are the called according to His purpose." *(Romans 8:28)* Mrs. Rice suffered several personal setbacks, including the tragic death of her husband only two years after they were married.

"At the time I was devastated," she told me. "I could not believe that God could work good out of such a happening. The wealth we had had was gone, and I had to go back to work. How I found my way to the Gibson Greeting Card Company in Cincinnati is nothing short of miraculous.

"But that was the key to my future, and what the Lord wanted me to do—write." She felt Divine Guidance in her life and it no doubt helped shape this verse:

Not by Chance or Happenstance

In our lives come many things
    to break the dull routine,
The things we had not planned on
    that happen unforeseen,
The unexpected little joys
    that are scattered on our way,
Success we did not count on
    or a rare, fulfilling day—
A catchy, lilting melody
    that makes us want to dance,
A nameless exaltation
    of enchantment and romance—
An unsought word of kindness,
    a compliment or two
That sets the eye to gleaming
    like crystal drops of dew,
The unplanned sudden meeting
    that comes with sweet surprise
And lights the heart with happiness
    like a rainbow in the skies,

Now some folks call it fickle fate
　　and some folks call it chance,
While others just accept it
　　as pleasant happenstance,
But no matter what you call it,
　　it didn't come without design,
For all our lives are fashioned
　　by the HAND THAT IS DIVINE—
And every happy happening
　　and every lucky break
Are little gifts from God above
　　that are ours to freely take.

One of the important tests of faith, Mrs. Rice believed, is our total openness to God's guidance. "Pray, listen, act" was her motto. She spoke of yielding to His sovereignty again and again, and is that not the real WHY of all good gifts?

A Christmas Prayer

Oh, Father up in heaven,
We have wandered far away,
From the Holy little Christ Child,
Who was born on Christmas Day.
And the Peace on Earth You promised,
We have been unmindful of,
Not believing we could find it
In a simple thing called love.
We've forgotten why You sent us
Jesus Christ, Your only Son,
And in arrogance and ignorance
It's OUR WILL not THINE BE DONE.
Oh, forgive us, heavenly Father,
Teach us how to be more kind,
So that we may judge all people
With our heart and not our mind.
And, oh God, in Thy great goodness,
May our guidance Christmas Night
Be the star the Wise Men followed—
Not a man-made satellite.

Chapter 3

The Who of Giving

Live Christmas Every Day

Christmas is more than a day
    at the end of the year,
More than a season
    of joy and good cheer,
Christmas is really
    God's pattern for living
To be followed all year
    by unselfish giving.
For the holiday season
    awakens good cheer
And draws us closer
    to those we hold dear,
And we open our hearts
    and find it is good
To live among men
    as we always should.
But as soon as the tinsel
    is stripped from the tree,
The spirit of Christmas
    fades silently
Into the background
    of daily routine,
And is lost in the whirl
    of life's busy scene.
And all unaware
    we miss and forego
The greatest blessing
    that mankind can know,

For if we lived Christmas
    every day, as we should,
And made it our aim
    to always do good,
We'd find the lost key
    to meaningful living
That comes not from getting,
    but from unselfish giving.
And we'd know the great joy
    of Peace upon Earth,
Which was the real purpose
    of our Saviour's birth,
For in the Glad Tidings
    of that first Christmas night,
God showed us THE WAY
    and the Truth and the Light!

One of the great joys of Helen Steiner Rice was giving away what she had been given. When a well-known songwriter offered to buy the rights to one of her poems so he could set it to music, she turned him down.

"You can't buy the poem, but you are welcome to use it without charge," she wrote. Then, she explained her philosophy about the verses that brought her so much acclaim.

"I more or less predicate my thinking on Hebrews 13:5, 'Be content with such things as ye have...' Since all our gifts are God-given and they do not belong to us, they only have worth when we share them with others. I am more interested in reaching people than making money. God gave me this gift and I am happy to return it to the world."

On a later occasion, she said, "I have never sought any publisher, nor am I concerned about or anxious for exposure. And I find this jet-propelled, commercially-crazed, sensation-saturated world increasingly abrasive. . . . I just think that what I am doing is between God and me. The majority of responsive hearts who read my things pass them along to other responsive hearts, and soon the chain of love reaches around the world."

To another correspondent, she wrote: "I never consider myself as a writer or author or poet. I just think of myself as another worker in God's 'vineyard,' and wonderful people all over the world are my co-workers.

"The loving interest that has come to my work is surely by divine design. I only share thoughts He has given me. All these things I say are just olden, golden truths that are constantly repeated down through the years. I am reminded of the majestic wisdom in Ecclesiastes *(1:9)*, 'The thing that hath been, it is that which shall be; and that which is done is that which shall be done; and there is no new thing under the sun.' The words of God's wisdom echo down through the ages, and the things I write were said long ago on ancient, ageless pages."

The Musings of a Thankful Heart

People everywhere in life
    from every walk and station
From every town and city
    and every state and nation,
Have given me so many things
    intangible and dear,
I couldn't begin to count them all
    or even make them clear.
I only know I owe so much
    to people everywhere
And when I put my thoughts in verse
    it's just my way to share

The musings of a thankful heart,
 a heart much like your own,
For nothing that I think or write
 is mine and mine alone...
So if you found some beauty
 in any word or line
It's just your soul's reflection
 in proximity with mine.

We All Need Words to Live By

We all need words to live by,
To inspire us and guide us,
Words to give us courage
When the trials of life betide us.
And the words that never fail us
Are the words of God above,
Words of comfort and of courage,
Filled with wisdom and with love—
They are ageless and enduring,
They have lived through generations,
There's no question left unanswered
In our Father's revelations—
And in this ever-changing world
God's words remain unchanged,
For though through countless ages
They've often been rearranged,
The truth that shines through all changes

Is just as bright today as when
Our Father made the universe
And breathed His life in men.
And the words of inspiration
That I write for you today
Are just old enduring truths
Said in a rhythmic way—
And if my "borrowed words of truth"
In some way touch your heart,
Then I am deeply thankful
To have had a little part
In sharing these God-given lines,
And I hope you'll share them, too,
With family, friends and loved ones
And all those dear to you.

Mrs. Rice gave witness to the depth of her faith in both word and deed. Not only did she encourage her readers to be more giving ("The joy of living is found in helping people, and as long as I am on earth, I hope I can help at least one person every day."), but she gave her time and talents and financial resources unreservedly. Churches, Christian agencies (like the Salvation Army) and young people were most often the beneficiaries of her generosity. Though her father's death while she was in high school deterred her from attending college, she helped many with their education.

Her charity was devoid of parochial bounds. Brought up as a Methodist in Lorain, Ohio, she was nevertheless non-denominational and interfaith when it came to charity. Her files were full of clippings detailing examples of people's kindnesses to each other. Mother Theresa and sisters of various Catholic orders were particular favorites of Mrs. Rice, because "they practice sacrificial love."

"What the world needs now is love, sweet love," goes the contemporary song. Helen would endorse those lyrics, but no doubt add "selfless, Christ-like love," because she believed that the great missing element in society today is a love that is willing to forgo personal gratification for the needs of others.

"Oh, how beautiful it was," she once told me, lamentingly, "when neighbors looked after neighbors. You didn't have to lock doors or worry about going for a walk at night."

Helen rued impolite behavior, thoughtless actions, destructiveness, disorder, litter, violence, apathy. Her dream was for a return to an earlier time when kindness, consideration and caring were the rule rather than the exception. Not surprisingly, she put her vision to meter:

The Candle of Faith

In this sick world of hatred
And violence and sin,
Where men renounce morals
And reject discipline,
We stumble in darkness,
Groping vainly for light
To distinguish the difference
Between wrong and right,
But dawn cannot follow
This night of despair
Unless faith lights a candle
In hearts everywhere,
And warmed by the flow
Our hatred melts away
And Love lights the path
To a peaceful new day.

Mrs. Rice once shared with me some paragraphs she had written at a time of discouragement in her life.

"These past few months I have been going through many hours of soul searching and walking through dark hours that come to us all. But I know God is behind the 'dark cloud' that engulfs me, and I must endure it until He removes the darkness, for this is not a destructive experience, but a constructive one. I am sure He is trying to awaken me to a new awareness of how to best serve Him...

"You see, what happens to us is not as important as how we take what happens to us. The real secret of happiness is not in doing what one likes, but in liking what one has to do. All real knowledge is gained along the pathway of experience, and how much you get depends on how much you give."

It is More Blessed to Give

The more you give,
    the more you get,
The more you laugh,
    the less you fret,
The more you do unselfishly,
    the more you live abundantly,
The more of everything you share,
    the more you'll always have to spare,
The more you love,
    the more you'll find
That life is good
    and friends are kind,
For only what we give away
    enriches us from day to day.

Corie, an aging widow who lived next door to me, was in poor health and of little means. She had once been active in her church, but now was confined to her apartment. "I'm of no use to anyone," she sighed. "I don't know why the Lord keeps me around. I have nothing to give."

"Nonsense," I told her, "everyone has something to give." Then we examined the ways in which she could still contribute. One way was with her prayers, which Corie had wrongly discounted. Another was by encouraging aging friends. There was a sickly woman who resided nearby; she practically *lived* for Corie's daily phone calls. And Corie discovered that the Lord needed her around. Mrs. Rice wrote a poem that spoke directly to Corie's need:

The End of the Road
is But a Bend in the Road

When we feel we have nothing left to give
    and we are sure that the "song has ended"
When our day seems over and the shadows fall
    and the darkness of night has descended,
Where can we go to find the strength
    to valiantly keep on trying,
Where can we find the hand that will dry
    the tears that the heart is crying—
There's but one place to go and that is to God
    and, dropping all pretense and pride,
We can pour out our problems without restraint
    and gain strength with Him at our side—
And together we stand at life's crossroads
    and view what we think is the end,
But God has a much bigger vision
    and He tells us it's ONLY A BEND—
For the road goes on and is smoother,
    and the "Pause in the song" is a "rest,"
And the part that's unsung and unfinished
    is the sweetest and richest and best—
So rest and relax and grow stronger,
    LET GO and LET GOD share your load,
Your work is not finished or ended,
    you've just come to a bend in the road.

I don't think the woman whom Christ praised, the widow who gave her last mite, felt depressed by her little gift. The lesson is not what one gives, but how. Saint Paul advised that those of us who sow sparingly shall reap sparingly, and those who sow bountifully shall reap bountifully. "...so let them give; not grudgingly, or of necessity: for God loveth a cheerful giver." *(II Corinthians 9:7)*

Too often, it seems to me, those of us who should be giving are still looking to receive. Gloria Gaither, who with her husband Bill, makes up one of the most talented gospel song-writing teams of our time, once told me this touching story:

It happened during Christmas break her senior year of college. "I had been on my own, enjoying my freedom and independence," Gloria told me, "so my thoughts were much more focused on myself and my world than others and theirs.

"When Christmas vacation came, I went home, but not to the place in which I'd grown up. Daddy had retired from the ministry and he and Mother had gone to live in a saltbox cottage they'd built at a Michigan lake.

"Grandma had died earlier that year and my sister had married, so she'd be spending Christmas with her husband and his folks. That left the three of us, and I could tell the moment I stepped inside the door that Mother and Daddy were depressed by the prospects of such an austere Christmas."

Gloria went on to describe the gala celebrations with aunts, uncles, cousins and friends that she experienced while growing up...the house a hubbub of activity: crackling logs on the fire, the heavenly aroma of homemade bread and cookies baking, the joyous sound of loved ones talking and singing.

"But this Christmas was to be different," she continued. "After an initial flurry of hugs and kisses, quiet descended upon us and we struggled to fill the silent gaps in our conversations. Finally Daddy suggested we go find a tree in the woods. One tradition we could keep was cutting our own Christmas tree.

"I put on my boots and happiest face and followed him out of the house. The land was wrapped in a white coat, and for a moment my heart skipped a beat as I trudged through the snow. For an instant it was like other childhood Christmases, but the sound of Daddy's whistling, a tuneless, off-key, under-the-breath whistle, brought the present back to mind. He always whistled when worried, and I could tell he was anxious.

" 'How 'bout this one?' he said pointing to a scraggly cedar.

" 'Beautiful,' I answered, showing ten times as much enthusiasm as I felt. But as I spoke and as Daddy began to wield his ax, I received a sudden insight. He was whistling his nervous whistle because he was afraid my Christmas would be spoiled. He was worried that I would be disappointed. Such love. Tears came to my eyes as I watched him fell the tree. And somewhere between then and the time it took us to carry it back to the house, I grew up... or at least I had the first feelings of adult responsibility."

Gloria finished her reminiscence by saying, "My parents

had filled me with so much 'good stuff.' Now I realized it was my turn to give some of it back, and for the rest of the holiday I tried. The result was that we had a marvelous Christmas, one that stands out as one of my most memorable and meaningful."

Helen Steiner Rice would have understood the spiritual growth Gloria Gaither discovered that Christmas because she often wrote about how Christ's love can transform us from takers to givers, from self-centered to others-centered, from hoarders of his blessings to sharers of them. In each of the following verses, Mrs. Rice pleads for self-denying love. Listen and you'll hear that underlying theme surface again and again.

God's Gift Divine

Love is enduring
And patient and kind,
It judges all things
With the heart not the mind,
And love can transform
The most commonplace
Into beauty and splendor
And sweetness and grace...
For love is unselfish,
Giving more than it takes,
And no matter what happens
Love never forsakes,
It's faithful and trusting
And always believing,
Guileless and honest
And never deceiving...
Yes, love is beyond
What man can define,
For love is immortal,
God's Gift is Divine!

Thy Will be Done

Do you want what you want when you want it?
Do you pray and expect a reply?
And when it's not instantly answered,
Do you feel that God passed you by?
Well, prayers that are prayed in this manner
Are really not prayers at all,
For you can't go to God in a hurry
And expect Him to answer your call...
For prayers are not meant for obtaining
What we selfishly wish to acquire,
For God in His wisdom refuses
The things that we wrongly desire.
Don't pray for freedom from trouble,
Or ask that life's trials pass you by,
Instead pray for strength and for courage
To meet life's "dark hours" and not cry
That God was not there when you called Him,
And He turned a deaf ear to your prayer
And just when you needed Him most,
He left you alone in despair...
Wake up! You are missing completely
The reason and purpose for prayer,
Which is really to keep us contented
That God holds us safe in His care.
And God only answers our pleadings
When He knows that our wants fill a need,
And whenever "our will" becomes "His will"
There is no prayer that God does not heed.

Widen My Vision, Lord

God, widen my vision so I may see
    the afflictions You have sent to me,
Not as a cross too heavy to bear
    that weighs me down in gloomy despair,
Not as something to hate and despise,
    but a gift of love sent in disguise.
Something to draw me closer to You
    to teach me patience and forebearance, too,
Something to show me more clearly the way
    to serve You and Love You more every day,
Something priceless and precious and rare
    that will keep me forever safe in Thy care,
Aware of the spiritual strength that is mine,
    if my selfish, small will is lost in Thine.

The Secret of Happiness

Everybody, everywhere, seeks happiness
    —it's true,
But finding it and keeping it
    seems difficult to do,
Difficult because we think
    that happiness is found
Only in the places where
    wealth and fame abound,
And so we go on searching
    in "palaces of pleasure"
Seeking recognition
    and monetary treasure,
Unaware that happiness
    is just a state of mind
Within the reach of everyone
    who takes time to be kind—
For in making others happy,
    we will be happy, too,
For the happiness you give away
    returns to shine on you.

Jesus told us "Thou shalt love the Lord thy God with all thy heart, and with all thy soul, and with all thy mind...and thy neighbor as thyself." *(Matthew 22:37, 39)* But the question has been raised: As we grow up, which comes first—love of God, love of neighbor or love of self? For most of us, the selfless love of our mothers and fathers is our earliest contact with real love. This physical and emotional closeness precedes our spiritual understanding of God's love.

Mrs. Rice said that she more fully understood her heavenly Father's love because she was blessed with such devoted parents, and that their sacrifices served as a bridge to accepting God and His love.

She made that link in this warm tribute to mothers:

A Mother's Love

A Mother's love is something
    that no one can explain,
It is made of deep devotion
    and of sacrifice and pain,
It is endless and unselfish
    and enduring come what may
For nothing can destroy it
    or take that love away...
It is patient and forgiving
    when all others are forsaking,
And it never fails or falters
    even when the heart is breaking...
It believes beyond believing
    when the world around condemns,

And it glows with all the beauty
    of the rarest, brightest gems...
It is far beyond defining,
    it defies all explanation,
And it still remains a secret
    like the mysteries of creation...
A many-splendored miracle
    man cannot understand
And another wondrous evidence
    of God's tender guiding hand.

Oh, those warm memories of gifts given by loving parents. Isn't it too bad that it takes most of us so long to see and appreciate their sacrifices. Often we have to become parents ourselves before we fully realize the degree and depth of our mothers' and fathers' struggles to give us their best, the "good stuff," Gloria Gaither called it.

Last year, I took my family back to Ohio, to Mother's for Christmas. It was extra special because included in our entourage was eight-month-old Jessica, our first grandchild. There's nothing like holding a new baby on your lap by the Christmas tree to help one understand the reason for celebration.

After the excitement of Christmas Day had passed, after the great mound of presents had been distributed and the tangle of wrapping paper disposed of, after the turkey had been picked bare, Mother and I sat in her living room, spinning memories about Christmases past.

We talked from twilight until there was no light, save that which came from the colored bulbs on her tree. Her childhood Christmases, Christmas Eve celebrations at Grandma Strayer's and Christmases when Dad was still alive all were replayed with warm nostalgia.

"That was the year Joy got married...That was the year Bud was in service....That was our first year in the Platt Street house..."

"The very first Christmas present I remember receiving," I mused at one point, "was the box of stuffed animals. There was a giraffe and a lion and a zebra and an orange camel with two humps..."

"You may remember the animals, but not the Christmas," Mother commented, "because you were too young." Then she went on to tell the story behind the creatures she had created out of old pieces of fabric.

"It was during the heart of the Depression and there was no money for Christmas presents," she began. "We barely had enough for food and rent.

"Then one day in the dime store you spotted some stuffed animals that stole your heart. They weren't much, probably only thirty or forty cents apiece, but then a quarter would buy three pounds of hamburger.

'Can't I have just the camel?' you begged.

'Not now, but maybe Santa will bring some animals for you,' I answered. I bit my tongue after saying it, because I knew there was no way your Dad or I could afford them.

"But you didn't forget and you had me write a letter to Santa asking for the animals, especially the camel with two humps. With tears in my eyes, I asked God to somehow help me find the money to buy the toys, 'So I don't disappoint a little boy.'

"Well, He didn't send the money, but I believe He sent me the inspiration. The idea came one evening only a few days before Christmas while I was doing some mending. I had come across a piece of orange material that reminded me of the color of the stuffed camel you wanted. Maybe I could make the animals, I thought. I was very young and not much of a seamstress, but I decided to try. I worked for hours that first night on the camel and finally gave up in tears. It looked more like a pig.

"But the next day, I tried again, and succeeded in making a zebra out of a piece of pillow casing that I striped with a black pen. After that I made a giraffe and a lion. Your Dad said they needed cages, so he fashioned some from shoe boxes.

"Finally Christmas Eve came. I had completed all the zoo collection except the camel with two humps. About eight o'clock I got out the piece of cloth and began sewing it together again. Then I ripped it out and started again. I don't know when I solved the problem, but at about 2:00 A.M. I put the last stitch in the camel and went to bed.

"The next morning you opened your packages with wide-eyed expectation...one stuffed animal after another. You were obviously pleased with the lion and the zebra and the giraffe, but I could tell you were looking for the camel. When at last you opened the package that held it, you let out a cry of joy I'll never forget."

I looked across the room at Mother's radiant face, lighted only by the lights from her tree. Reflecting off one cheek was a tear that spoke more than words of how much that memory meant to her. It is a picture I won't ever forget.

It has been my observation that the most enthusiastic givers in life are the real livers of life. They experience the soul-joy that comes from responding with the heart rather than the head.

Too often, we can talk ourselves out of generous responses. We reason that the need isn't great enough or that others are more worthy. Our procrastination causes us to miss a great opportunity and an even greater blessing.

I tried to speak to this problem once in a poem:

Don't Wait

Don't wait for the perfect season
    to give your love away,
Don't wait for the ideal reason
    your thankfulness to pay,
For time has a way of fleeing,
    of quickly skittering by,
Of strangely evanescing
    like cloudy wisps on high.
Roses don't last forever,
    they lose their nubile red,
Just as deeds unacted,
    just as thoughts unsaid.
The Gift of Life is not book-end-less,
    finite, we, He did create,
TODAY He bids us send our love,
    tomorrow may be too late.

—FB

One of the things that always impressed me about Mrs. Rice was how clearly she had her priorities in order. She knew that people always come before things, and God before all. You cannot serve God AND mammon.

Always, her poems focused on the lasting over the passing, the timeless over the temporal. "Don't dwell on your shortcomings," she advised. "You have all you need to serve Him. Make the most of what He's provided. Focus on others. Give them your love and attention and you will be blessed beyond anything you can imagine."

A Thankful Heart

Take nothing for granted,
 for whenever you do,
The joy of enjoying
 is lessened for you—
For we rob our own lives
 much more than we know
When we fail to respond
 or in any way show
Our thanks for the blessings
 that daily are ours—
The warmth of the sun,
 the fragrance of flowers,
The beauty of twilight,
 the freshness of dawn,
The coolness of dew
 on a green velvet lawn,

The kind little deeds,
    so thoughtfully done,
The favors of friends
    and the love that someone
Unselfishly gives us
    in a myriad of ways,
Expecting no payment
    and no words of praise.
Oh, great is our loss
    when we no longer find
A thankful response
    to things of this kind,
For the joy of enjoying,
    and the fullness of living,
Are found in the heart
    that is filled with thanksgiving.

Chapter 4

The Where of Giving

Brighten the Corner Where You Are

We cannot all be famous
    or listed in "Who's Who,"
But every person great or small
    has important work to do,
For seldom do we realize
    the importance of small deeds,
Or to what degree of greatness
    unnoticed kindness leads—
For it's not the big celebrity
    in a world of fame and praise,
But it's doing unpretentiously
    in undistinguished ways,
The work that God assigned for us,
    unimportant as it seems,
That makes our task outstanding
    and brings reality to dreams—
So do not sit and idly wish
    for wider, newer dimensions,
Where you can put in practice
    your many good intentions—
But at the spot God placed you
    begin at once to do
Little things to brighten up
    the lives surrounding you,
For if everybody brightened up
    the spot on which they're standing,

89

By being more considerate
    and a little less demanding,
This dark cold world would very soon
    eclipse the Evening Star,
If everybody brightened up
    the corner where they are.

I am a collector of Bibles—old ones and new ones. On my bookshelves are many different translations as well as many guides and interpretative volumes about the Bible. But my favorite volumes are copies that belonged to loved ones such as my Grandmother Strayer and my wife, Shirley, when she was a teenager.

Notes in the margins and at the end of meaningful passages are particularly interesting and revealing. My mother, a long-time student and teacher of the Bible, is a heavy annotator of Scripture and reading the comments in her well-worn Bible is like attending one of her lively classes. She told me recently that she wanted me to have her latest Bible, "After I close it for the last time." I told her I'd see that her great-grandchildren read it.

Another treasured Bible on my bookshelf once belonged to Helen Steiner Rice. In it she underscored and page-marked passages that she had apparently found significant. Leafing through it the other day, I came upon some verses in Proverbs she had checked.

They read: "Trust in the Lord with all thine heart; and lean not unto thine own understanding.

"In all thy ways acknowledge him, and he shall direct thy paths.

"Be not wise in thine own eyes: fear the Lord, and depart from evil...

"Honour the Lord with thy substance, and with the first fruits of all thine increase. *(Proverbs 3: 5-9)*

It is not surprising to me that these verses were particularly meaningful to Mrs. Rice (she loved Psalms and Proverbs), because they encompass several themes she returned to again and again: trust, obedience, God's guidance, His blessings, generosity.

Once she told how the Bible's truths had become more vivid to her as she had grown older. "I see how God has tried to shape me," she said. "How He has tried to take me and break me until I become what He wants."

More of Thee, Less of Me

Take me and break me and make me, dear God,
Just what you want me to be—
Give me the strength to accept what you send,
And eyes with the vision to see
All the small arrogant ways that I have
And the vain things that I do,
Make me aware that I'm often concerned
More with myself than with You.
Uncover before me my weakness and greed
And help me to search deep inside,
So I may discover how easy it is
To be selfishly lost in my pride—
And then in Thy goodness and mercy
Look down on this weak, erring one,

And tell me that I am forgiven
For all I've so willfully done.
And teach me to humbly start following
The path that the dear Saviour trod,
So I'll find at the end of life's journey,
A home in the City of God.

It is not surprising that Mrs. Rice's foolproof prescription for a sick soul or aching heart was the Psalms. She wrote about her favorite in this often-quoted poem.

There's Peace and Calm in the 23rd Psalm

With the Lord as your shepherd
    you have all that you need,
For, if you follow in His footsteps
    wherever He may lead,
He will guard and guide and keep you
    in His loving, watchful care,
And when traveling in "dark valleys"
    your Shepherd will be there...
His goodness is unfailing,
    His kindness knows no end,
For the Lord is a Good Shepherd
    on whom you can depend...
So when your heart is troubled,
    you'll find quiet, peace and calm,
If you open up the Bible
    and just read this treasured Psalm.

Frequently, Mrs. Rice petitioned God in her prayer-poems for better understanding, greater insight, clearer vision and a deeper sensitivity to the needs of others. Like the Minute Men of the Revolutionary War, Mrs. Rice felt Christians should be ready to serve whenever and wherever God asked them.

It was her belief that too often those of us who pray, "Here am I, send me," don't really mean it, and instead of acting when opportunities arise we often find excuses to avoid involvement. She was fond of some verses in Matthew that read:

"For I was an hungered, and ye gave me meat: I was thirsty, and ye gave me drink: I was a stranger and ye took me in: Naked, and ye clothed me: I was sick and ye visited me: I was in prison, and ye came unto me. Then shall the righteous answer him, saying, 'Lord when saw we thee an hungered, and fed thee? or thirsty, and gave thee drink? When saw we thee a stranger, and took thee in? or naked, and clothed thee? Or when saw we thee sick, or in prison, and came unto thee?' And the King shall answer and say unto them, 'Verily I say unto you, Inasmuch as ye have done it unto one of the least of these my brethren, ye have done it unto me.'" *(Matthew 25: 35-40)*

Listen closely to the wise words of Mrs. Rice that point to where she felt we should focus our faith:

Healing the Wounds of Others

Let me not live a life that's free
From the things that draw me close to Thee,
For how can I ever hope to heal
The wounds of others I do not feel—
If my eyes are dry and I never weep,
How do I know when the hurt is deep,
If my heart is cold and it never bleeds,
How can I tell what my brother needs,
For when ears are deaf to the beggar's pleas,
And we close our eyes and refuse to see,
And we steel our hearts and harden our mind,
And we count it a weakness whenever we're kind,
We are no longer following the Father's way,
Or seeking His guidance from day to day—
For without crosses to carry and burdens to bear,
We dance through a life that is frothy and fair,
And "chasing the rainbow" we have no desire
For roads that are rough and realms that are higher—
So spare me no heartache or sorrow, dear Lord,
For the heart that is hurt reaps the richest reward,
And God enters the heart that is broken in sorrow
As He opens the door to a brighter tomorrow,
For only through tears can we recognize
The suffering that lies in another's eyes.

The Faith to Believe

What must I do
    to insure peace of mind?
Is the answer I'm seeking
    too hard to find?
How can I know
    what God wants me to be?
How can I tell
    what's expected of me?
Where can I go
    for guidance and aid
To help me correct
    the errors I've made
The answer is found
    in doing three things,
And great is the gladness
    that doing them brings...
Do justice, love kindness,
    walk humbly with God,
For with these three things
    as your rule and your rod,
All things worth having
    are yours to achieve
If you follow God's words
    and have faith to believe.

Stir Us With Compassion

Oh, God, renew our spirit and make us more aware
That our future is dependent on sacrifice and prayer,
Forgive us our transgressions and revive our
     faith anew,
So we may all draw closer to each other and to you...
Stir us with compassion and raise our
     standards higher
And take away our lust for power and make our
     one desire
To be a shining symbol of all that's great and good,
As you lead us in our struggle toward newfound
     brotherhood.

A Prayer for Guidance

God, grant us the grace as another year starts
　　　to use all the hours of our days,
Not for our own selfish interest,
　　　our own willful, often wrong ways,
But teach us to take time for prayer,
　　　and to find time for listening to You,
So each day is spent well and wisely,
　　　doing what You most want us to do.

Where should we place our emphasis when it comes to giving? The answer is obvious that we all have different gifts and that God directs we use them differently. One day I was having lunch with two friends who have spent their lives giving: Norman Vincent Peale and his wife Ruth. I don't remember much of what we were talking about but at one point Ruth said that she liked the idea that "we should bloom where we are planted."

I wrote her words down in my little black book, and later shaped them into this little verse.

Bloom Where You Are Planted

Though the ground you've been given is rocky,
    a less than ideal plot,
No good will come from complaining,
    o'er your less than ideal lot
Roll up your sleeves and dig in,
    make the best of what you've been given,
Turn your deserts into gardens verdant,
    it's the way of successful livin'.
Few joys will give you more pleasure,
    few rewards rival or match,
The thrill that comes from creating
    something glorious from scratch,
Now the Lord may someday present you
    with a place far greater than now,
Green pastures that stretch on forever,
    fields that have not seen a plow,
But don't wait for a dreamland harvest,
    don't pass up the crop at hand,
Opportunity's a fickle dayflower,
    make the most of your God-given land,
Bloom where you are planted,
    work today as if it's your last,
The Lord will richly bless you
    and you'll never regret the past.

—FB
99

Mrs. Rice believed in the "no pain, no gain," school of thought. "Nobody finds carrying their cross easy," she once wrote, "but when we pick up our cross and carry it we grow in grace. We also grow closer to God and to others...and your cross becomes your crown."

"For me to live is Christ, and to die is gain," Paul wrote to the Philippians *(1:21)*. The verse was a particularly poignant one for Mrs. Rice.

"None of us can fully understand the impenetrable mystery of death," she wrote once. "However, it is through death that we come closer to God and each other.

"Great Nature just opens up her arms and receives back the fleshly garments that clothe our loved ones' souls. And they rise unencumbered to meet God, and they wait for us in that place where there are no separations and time is not counted by years.

"Of course, to me death is just another step along the pathway of life, and it gives so much meaning and purpose to all living. It gives us the great joy of heading happily towards the ultimate goal of every Christian, and that is to live forever in the unending sunshine of God's love!

"It is hard to reconcile ourselves to a loss when God asks us to give up someone young and in mid-career with abundant years stretching ahead of them, for to have a life so suddenly silenced is beyond our understanding.

"But there is something brave and beautiful in passing at this high peak' while standing on tiptoe, going into new fields of usefulness without ever having to lessen their zest for living.

We know that Christ's coming into this world makes our leave-taking only the beginning of a new life that is without end."

One of her most popular poems about the loss of loved ones was written at the time of her mother's death.

When I Must Leave You

When I must leave you
    for a little while,
Please do not grieve
    and shed wild tears
And hug your sorrow
    to you through the years,
But start out bravely
    with a gallant smile;
And for my sake
    and in my name
Live on and do
    all things the same,
Feed not your loneliness
    on empty days
But fill each waking hour
    in useful ways,
Reach out your hand
    in comfort and in cheer
And I in turn will comfort you
    and hold you near;

And never, never
      be afraid to die,
For I am waiting
      for you in the sky!

Mrs. Rice also spoke of her belief in life beyond the grave in these "story" poems that follow:

The Message of the Fire Lily

The crackling flames rise skyward
      as the waving grain is burned,
But from the fire on the veld
      a great truth can be learned.
For the green and living hillside
      becomes a funeral pyre,
As all the grass across the veld
      is swallowed by the fire.
What yesterday was living,
      today is dead and still,
But soon a breathless miracle
      takes place upon the hill.
For, from the blackened ruins
      there arises life anew,
And scarlet lilies lift their heads
      where once the veld grass grew.

And so again the mystery
of life and death is wrought,
And man can find assurance
in this soul-inspiring thought,
That from a bed of ashes
the fire lilies grew,
And from the ashes of our lives
God resurrects us, too.

The Praying Hands

The *"Praying Hands"* are much, much more
than just a work of art,
They are the "soul's creation"
of a deeply thankful heart—
They are a *Priceless Masterpiece*
that love alone could paint,
And they reveal the selflessness
of an unheralded saint—
These hands so scarred and toilworn,
tell the story of a man
Who sacrificed his talent
in accordance with God's Plan—
For in God's Plan are many things
man cannot understand,
But we must trust God's judgment
and be guided by His Hand—

Sometimes He asks us to give up
　　our dreams of happiness,
Sometimes we must forego our hopes
　　of fortune and success—
Not all of us can triumph
　　or rise to heights of fame,
And many times *What Should Be Ours*,
　　goes to *Another Name*—
But he who makes a sacrifice,
　　so another may succeed,
Is indeed a true disciple
　　of our blessed Saviour's creed—
For when we "give ourselves away"
　　in sacrifice and love,
We are "laying up rich treasures"
　　in God's kingdom up above—
And hidden in gnarled, toilworn hands
　　is the truest *Art of Living*,
Achieved alone by those who've learned
　　the *"Victory of Giving"*—
For any sacrifice on earth,
　　made in the dear Lord's name,
Assures the giver of a place
　　In heaven's Hall of Fame.

The Legend of the Raindrop

The legend of the raindrop
    has a lesson for us all
As it trembled in the heavens
    questioning whether it should fall—
For the glistening raindrop argued
    to the genie of the sky,
"I am beautiful and lovely
    as I sparkle here on high,
And hanging here I will become
    part of the rainbow's hue
And I'll shimmer like a diamond
    for all the world to view."
But the genie told the raindrop,
    "Do not hesitate to go,
For you will be more beautiful
    if you fall to earth below,
For you will sink into the soil
    and be lost a while from sight,
But when you reappear on earth,
    you'll be looked on with delight;
For you will be the raindrop
    that quenched the thirsty ground
And helped the lovely flowers
    to blossom all around,
And in your resurrection
    you'll appear in queenly clothes
With the beauty of the lily
    and the fragrance of the rose;

105

Then, when you wilt and wither,
　　you'll become part of the earth
And make the soil more fertile
　　and give new flowers birth."
For there is nothing ever lost
　　or eternally neglected,
For everything God ever made
　　Is always resurrected;
So trust God's all-wise wisdom
　　and doubt the Father never,
For in His heavenly kingdom
　　There is nothing lost forever.

Chapter 5

The What of Giving

What is Christmas?

Is it just a day at the end of the year?
A gay holiday filled with merry good cheer?
A season for presents—both taking and giving?
A time to indulge in the pleasures of living?
Are we lost in a meaningless, much-muddled daze
That covers our minds like a gray autumn haze?
Have we closed our hearts to God and His love?
And turned our eyes from "the bright Star above?"
Oh, Father, in heaven, renew and restore
The real, true meaning of Christmas once more,
So we can feel in our hearts again
That Peace on Earth, Good Will to Men
Is still a promise that man can claim
If he but seeks it in Thy name.

The stumping question most frequently heard by shoppers at Christmastime is, "What can I get her or him?" The problem is made more difficult if the recipient of the gift doesn't really have any pressing needs. An indication of our general affluence can be measured by the number of times advertisers use the line, "For the man or woman who has everything." Obviously, such commercials were not intended for the estimated two-thirds of the world that goes to sleep hungry every night.

But there are other unfulfilled needs at Christmas that fall under the heading of spiritual. My friend, Joni Eareckson Tada, once told me about a personal need of hers the first Christmas following the diving accident that left her a quadriplegic, paralyzed from the neck down. The contrast between the warm family celebration she had had at age sixteen and the depressing one she faced a year later left her full of despair and self pity.

"I was in the hospital as Christmas approached, unable to participate in the excitement of the holidays," she recalled. "One of the joys of Christmas for me had always been shopping for the perfect gift, the absolute 'best' gift for everyone on my list. One Christmas I looked for days before I found just the right sweater for my sister Jay, light peach, size 36 with embroidery at the neck. For Mother, the ideal gift might have been a special dress; for my boyfriend, maybe a hand-tooled belt; for Dad, a fancy horse bridle with silver trim. It was exhausting but unbelievable fun to see their faces on Christmas Eve when we opened presents.

"But I had forfeited such fun because of my physical limitations, and I found myself feeling lower than I had in months. The thought that I would have nothing to give at Christmas filled me with growing frustration and one day I blurted out, 'God, You have ruined everything!'

"I blamed Him for my predicament," Joni recalled, "and I shed a lot of tears thinking about how awful the coming Christmas was going to be, and it would have been a bad one had not something happened to change it.

"A friend who came to the hospital every day often read to me from the Bible—I couldn't hold a book myself. One day he turned to the third chapter of John and repeated those familiar words, 'For God so loved the world, that He gave His only begotten Son...' For the first time, I realized that God's best gift, the one that proved forever just how much He cared for us, was a gift of Himself, the gift of His Son. Likewise, I saw that my best gift to Him and to those I loved was myself. And in that instant I knew what I must do.

"The next day when it came time for occupational therapy, something I'd entered into only halfheartedly before, I asked the therapist to bring me one of the mud-colored candy dishes like the ones the other patients had been decorating. Next I asked for a paintbrush and some red and green paints."

Then, Joni described how a brush was placed in her mouth for the first time and how she began the process of learning to

direct it. "Few brush marks landed where I aimed them...
green was slopped where I wanted red and vice versa.

"The result," she remembers with a smile, "was something comparable to what a kindergartner might do. But it was the best I could do and I painted more candy dishes in the days just before Christmas.

"Finally, when six were finished, I had them put in a kiln and glazed. Then, they were wrapped in Christmas paper and given to loved ones as my presents. They weren't expensive, store-bought gifts like the ones I usually gave and they weren't pretty gifts. But I knew they were my *best* gifts because they were *self* gifts."

Joni's story illustrates well the point I once tried to make about giving your best:

Ours is Not to Reason Why

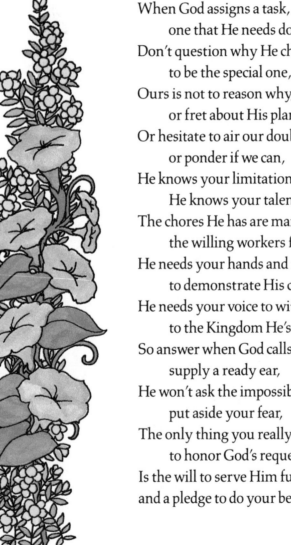

When God assigns a task,
　　one that He needs done,
Don't question why He chose you
　　to be the special one,
Ours is not to reason why,
　　or fret about His plan,
Or hesitate to air our doubts,
　　or ponder if we can,
He knows your limitations,
　　He knows your talents, too,
The chores He has are many,
　　the willing workers few,
He needs your hands and feet,
　　to demonstrate His caring,
He needs your voice to witness
　　to the Kingdom He's preparing,
So answer when God calls you,
　　supply a ready ear,
He won't ask the impossible,
　　put aside your fear,
The only thing you really need
　　to honor God's request,
Is the will to serve Him fully,
　　and a pledge to do your best.

　　　　　　　　　—FB

But when the subject is giving one's best few words speak more challengingly than those of that old evangelical hymn, "Give of Your Best to the Master."

Give of your best to the Master;
Naught else is worthy His love;
He gave Himself for your ransom,
Gave up His glory above;
Laid down His life without murmur,
You from sin's ruin to save;
Give Him your heart's adoration,
Give Him the best that you have...

Mrs. Rice's poetic message for those who would ask the question "What can I give?" was restated in many different ways, but unqualified love was always the heart of her answer.

"Love is indeed a many-splendored thing." she once wrote. "When it is given and returned, it enriches both the lover and the beloved. Nothing in the world is too difficult or impossible, and wanting to do something for someone you love takes all the burden out of it...

"God is love, and He made the human heart capable of love so that we might glimpse heaven and experience His divine touch. And in the wonder and awe of this glory, we feel His nearness and realize that it is He, and He alone, who can make love eternal..."

Such lasting love is the subject of the following poems:

His Unconditional Love

It's amazing and incredible,
But it's true as it can be,
God loves and understands us all
And that means you and me.
His grace is all sufficient
For both the young and old,
For the lonely and the timid,
For the brash and for the bold.
His love knows no exceptions,
So never feel excluded,
No matter who or what you are
Your name has been included.
And no matter what your past has been,
Trust God to understand,
And no matter what your problem is
Just place it in His hand.
For in all of our unloveliness
This great God loves us still,
He loved us since the world began,
And what's more, He always will.

Where There is Love

Where there is love, the heart is light,
Where there is love, the day is bright,
Where there is love, there is a song
To help when things are going wrong,
Where there is love, there is a smile
To make all things seem more worthwhile,
Where there is love, there's quiet peace,
A tranquil place where turmoils cease,
Love changes darkness into light,
And makes the heart take wingless flight,
Oh, blest are they who walk in love,
They also walk with God above—
And when man walks with God again,
There shall be peace on earth for men.

A Child's Faith

"Jesus loves me, this I know,
For the BIBLE tells me so"
Little children ask no more,
For love is all they're looking for,
And in a small child's shining eyes
The FAITH of all the ages lies
And tiny hands and tousled heads
That kneel in prayer by little beds
Are closer to the dear Lord's heart
And of His Kingdom more a part
Than we who search, and never find,
The answers to our questioning mind.
For FAITH in things we cannot see
Requires a child's simplicity
For, lost in life's complexities,

We drift upon uncharted seas
And slowly FAITH disintegrates
While wealth and power accumulates—
And the more man learns, the less he knows,
And the more involved his thinking grows
And, in his arrogance and pride,
No longer is man satisfied
To place his confidence and love
With childlike FAITH in God above—
Oh, Father, grant once more to men
A simple childlike FAITH again
And, with a small child's trusting eyes,
May all men come to realize
That FAITH alone can save man's soul
And lead him to a HIGHER GOAL.

Keep Christ in Your Christmas

Christmas is a season for joy and merrymaking,
A time for gifts and presents—for giving and
    for taking,
A festive, friendly happy time when everyone is gay,
And cheer, good will and laughter are part of
    Christmas Day,
For God wants us to be happy on the birthday of
    His Son,
And that is why this season is such a joyous one,
For long ago the angels rejoiced at Bethlehem,
And down through the ages we have followed
    after them.

But in our celebrations of merriment and mirth,
Let us not forget the miracle of the holy Christ
    Child's birth,
For in our gay festivities it's so easy to lose sight
Of the baby in the manger on that holy silent night,
For Christmas in this modern world is a very
    different scene
From the stable and the Christ Child so peaceful
    and serene,

And we often miss the mighty meaning and lose the
    greater glory
Of the holy little Christ Child and the blessed
    Christmas story
If we don't keep Christ in Christmas and make His
    love a part
Of all the joy and happiness that fill our home
    and heart.

For without the holy Christ Child what is Christmas
    but a day
That is filled with empty pleasures that will only
    pass away.
But by keeping Christ in Christmas we are helping
    to fulfill
The glad tidings of the angels: Peace on earth to men,
    good will,
And the Father up in heaven looking down on earth
    will say,
You have kept Christ in your Christmas, now I'll keep
    you all the way.

His Matchless Love

God's love is like an island
In life's ocean vast and wide,
A peaceful, quiet shelter
From the restless, rising tide,

God's love is like an anchor
When the angry billows roll,
A mooring in the storms of life,
A stronghold for the soul,

God's love is like a fortress
And we seek protection there,

When the waves of tribulation
Seem to drown us in despair,

God's love is like a harbor
Where our souls can find sweet rest
From the struggle and the tension
Of life's fast and futile quest,

God's love is like a beacon,
Burning bright with faith and prayer,
And through the changing scenes of life
We can find a haven there.

Chapter 6

The How of Giving

How to Find His Blessed Assurance

In the wondrous Christmas story
    a troubled world can find
Blessed reassurance
    and enduring peace of mind—
For though we grow discouraged
    in the world we're living in,
There is comfort just in knowing
    that God triumphed over sin
By sending us His only Son
    to live among us here,
So He might know and understand
    man's loneliness and fear,
And for our soul's salvation
    Christ was born and lived and died,
For life became immortal
    when God's Son was crucified,
And the Christ Child's Resurrection
    was God's way of telling men
That in Christ we are Eternal
    and in Him we live again,
And to know that life is endless
    puts new purpose in our days
And fills our hearts with joyous songs
    of hope and love and praise,
For to know that through the Christ Child
    our spirits were redeemed
And that God has stored up treasures
    beyond all that man has dreamed,

Is a promise that is priceless
     and it's ours if we but say
That "in so far as in us lies"
     we will follow in His way,
For God our heavenly Father
     and Christ, His only Son,
Will forgive us our transgressions
     and the misdeeds we have done,
If we but yield our hearts to God
     and ask but one reward,
The joy of walking daily
     in the footsteps of the Lord.

*L*ike saying "I love you," some of us have trouble putting our convictions about giving into actions. We know as Christians we should be more giving, more active in demonstrating our faith, but something holds us back.

"I don't have time to do everything I should," is a common excuse. But studies of human behavior suggest that people do find time for the really important things in their lives. Apathy has been suggested as one of the strongest reasons we aren't more charitable; inertia another. But whatever we call it, turning our backs on need is self-serving rather than Christ-serving. And isn't how we serve Christ a measure of our spiritual maturity? Too often, we look for an immediate pay-off from our beneficence and when gratitude is not forthcoming we are disappointed and/or hurt. In truth, giving, like virtue, should be its own reward.

There was a famous Jewish philosopher-physician-astronomer-rabbi by the name of Moses ben Maimon, known as Maimonides (1135-1204), who defined giving in what he called a "Golden Ladder of Charity." There were eight steps on the ladder and each represented a higher level of giving. A review of them is instructive for all of us.

1) The lowest degree is to give—but with reluctance or regret. This is a gift of the hand but not the heart.

2) To give cheerfully, but not proportionately to the distress of the suffering.

3) To give cheerfully, and proportionately, but not until we are solicited.

4) To give cheerfully, proportionately and even unsolicited, but to put the gift in the poor man or woman's hand, thereby inflicting upon him or her the painful experience of receiving charity.

5) To give in such a way that the distressed may receive the bounty and know their benefactor, without the benefactor knowing the recipient. It was once the practice of benefactors to tie money in the corners of their cloaks so that the poor could take a gift unperceived.

6) To know the object of our bounty, but remain unknown to the recipient. It was once the practice of people to deliver their charitable gifts to a needy one's dwelling, taking care that the giver remain unknown.

7) More meritorious still; to bestow charity in such a way that the benefactor may not know the relieved persons, or they the name of their benefactor.

8) The most meritorious of all; to anticipate charity by preventing poverty; namely, to assist our brother by a gift or a loan; or by teaching him a trade, or by putting him in the way of business so that he can earn an honest living and not be forced to hold up his hand for charity.

So how should we give? Privately and graciously. When we give our *best* selves and expect no reward we are climbing the ladder.

Mrs. Rice believed that the gift of friendship was one of the most valuable things we have to offer, because true friends commit themselves to each other and make a silent pledge to be available in times of need.

The Gift of Friendship

Friendship is a priceless gift
That cannot be bought or sold,
But its value is far greater
Than a mountain of gold—
For gold is cold and lifeless,
It can neither see nor hear,
And in the time of trouble
It is powerless to cheer,
It has no ears to listen,
No heart to understand,
It cannot bring you comfort,
Or reach out a helping hand,
So when you ask God for a gift,
Be thankful if He sends,
Not diamonds, pearls or riches,
But the love of real true friends.

Parents can set an example of giving for their children, by demonstrating not only a charitable spirit, but a graciousness and gratitude when others honor them with their gifts, be they material or spiritual.

To teach the art of giving and receiving should be a high priority for parents. I never think of that responsibility without being reminded of Moss Hart's experience when his father took him on a Christmas gift-buying mission. The famous playwright described his father as a rather stern man, bent down by the pressures of making a living for his family.

But one year as Christmas drew near, the elder Hart told his son to put on his hat and coat and come with him. Moss did as he was told and followed his father along a street not far from their New York City apartment where vendors had set up tables featuring hundreds of toys to delight children.

Together, the Harts walked along inspecting the merchandise. Occasionally, without a word, the father would inspect an item and then present it for his son's approval. And Moss shook his head, no, it was not what he wanted. But if Moss saw something exciting, he would point to it for his father's approval, and then the ritual was reversed and senior Hart would shake his head no.

As they neared the end of the line of toy-laden tables, Moss said that he suddenly realized his father's dilemma; he had been trying to buy him a Christmas present, but had only a small amount of money. Anything desirable was too expensive. So, empty-handed, the two of them trudged home, and that was as close to a gift that Moss got that Christmas.

It would seem their mission had been a failure, Moss reported retrospectively, but in fact it was a highpoint in their relationship. Looking back, he saw the incident in its true light: a father trying desperately to communicate his love. The playwright said he counted it as the time in his life that he felt closest to his father.

Love, as Henry Drummond told us, is the greatest thing in the world, and the gift of one's self—even when proffered haltingly and less than perfectly—is a precious, priceless thing.

Only God's Love is Forever

Everything in life is passing
    and whatever we possess
Cannot endure forever,
    but ends in nothingness,
For there are no safety boxes
    nor vaults that can contain
The possessions we've collected
    and desire to retain...
For only in God's Kingdom
    do our treasures last forever,
So use the word "forever"
    with sanctity and love,
For nothing is forever,
    but the love of God above.

While helping Mrs. Rice write her life's story, *In the Vineyard of the Lord,* I spent many hours reading letters she'd collected in her files. They revealed an army of friends that she had made through her correspondence. Some of her pen-pals were famous, but most were common folks, those she felt that God loved the most, "because He made so many of them."

Most writers who attain Mrs. Rice's popularity are inundated with mail, and they find it an enormous problem answering all the questions and requests that come to them. Not Mrs. Rice. She never complained about the heavy load, but answered her mail with buoyant enthusiasm. Hearing from readers that her poems were loved and appreciated was, she confided, the best payment she could receive.

Some letters told of bereavements that she had helped her correspondents through. Others spoke of illnesses she had helped them weather, of disappointments and defeats she had helped them overcome, of loneliness she had helped them deal with, and with infirmities of aging that she had helped them accept.

Mrs. Rice's responses were not the perfunctory "thank you" that might be expected. No, they were often lengthy, filled with commiseration, counsel, encouragement and prayers. It was not uncommon for her letters to turn into spontaneous verse. Her joyous spirit had trouble sticking to straight prose and her correspondents were often treated to an original couplet or two of rhyme.

"You'll never grow old, for you've so much to give/You'll always be young, you know how to live!" she wrote one admirer.

To a letter writer who was worried about the state of world affairs, Mrs. Rice advised:

I know not what the future holds,
But I know God holds my hand,
And with God Almighty leading,
I don't need to understand.

To another she encouraged:

There is one thing I know to be true,
No one is more qualified to do your job than you,
You're a lovely lady, smart, kind and sweet,
And that combination's mighty hard to beat.

Recently in my file, I found this little spirit brightener that she had sent me one Easter: "May He continue bestowing His blessings on you, and keep you writing the way that you do."

When someone wrote seeking her thoughts on life after death, adding the aside that he was assuming she did in fact believe in an afterlife, Mrs. Rice shot off this record-straightening missive:

"First of all, I am not assuming that there is a life after death, I *know* there is. And every day I am one step nearer eternal life, and I intend to graduate to glory without questioning its existence...

"The Creator got me safely here, and He will take me safely back without my knowing the particulars. If we could answer all the questions about life after death, there would be no need for faith...The ways of the Creator are unfathomable, and I am too busy trying to walk in His footsteps to spend any time on what eternity holds for me."

Such absolute truth, such positive affirmation, such unqualified certitude about matters of faith are repeatedly reflected in Helen Steiner Rice's faith-engendering messages—priceless words that were her response to His Priceless Gift.

Keep on Believing

There's no cloud too dark
  for God's light to penetrate,
If we keep on believing
  and have faith enough to wait.

On the Wings of Prayer

Just close your eyes and open your heart,
And feel your worries and cares depart,
Just yield yourself to the Father above
And let Him hold you secure in His love,
For life on earth grows more involved
With endless problems that can't be solved,
But God only asks us to do our best,
Then He will take over and finish the rest,
So when you are tired, discouraged and blue,
There's always one door that is open to you,
And that is the door to the house of prayer,

And you'll find God waiting to meet you there…
And the house of prayer is no farther away,
Than the quiet spot where you kneel and pray,
For the heart is a temple when God is there,
As we place ourselves in His loving care.

When God Comes Closest

Nature's greatest forces
 Are found in quiet things,
Like softly falling snowflakes
 Drifting down on angels' wings,
Or petals dropping soundlessly
 From a lovely full-blown rose,
So God comes closest to us
 When our souls are in repose…
So let us plan with prayerful care
 To always allocate
A certain portion of each day
 To be still and meditate…
For when everything is quiet
 And we're lost in meditation,
Our soul is then preparing
 For a deeper dedication
That will make it wholly possible
 To quietly endure
The violent world around us,
 For in God we are secure

Take Your Burdens to the Lord

The Lord is our salvation
And our strength in every fight,
Our redeemer and protector,
Our eternal, guiding light,
He has promised to sustain us,
He's our refuge from all harms,
And underneath this refuge
Are His everlasting arms—
So cast your burdens on Him,
Seek His counsel when distressed,
And go to Him for comfort
When you're lonely and oppressed.

There is Cause for Rejoicing

May the holy remembrance of that first
    Christmas Day,
Be our reassurance that Christ is not far away,
For on Christmas He came to walk here on earth,
So let us find joy in the news of His birth,
And let us find comfort and strength for each day
In knowing that Christ walked this same earthly way,
He knows all our needs, and hears every prayer,
And He keeps all His children safe in His care,
So once more at Christmas, let the whole
    world rejoice
In the knowledge He answers every prayer that
    we voice.

Let Not Your Heart be Troubled

Whenever I am troubled
    and lost in deep despair
I bundle all my troubles up
    and go to God in prayer.

I tell Him I am heartsick
    and lost and lonely, too,
That my mind is deeply burdened
    and I don't know what to do.

But I know He stilled the tempest
    and calmed the angry sea
And I humbly ask if in His love
    He'll do the same for me.

And then I just keep quiet
    and think only thoughts of peace
And if I abide in stillness
    my restless murmurings cease.

Helen Steiner Rice's Daily Prayer

Bless me, heavenly Father,
    forgive my erring ways,
Grant me strength to serve Thee,
    put purpose in my days...
Give me understanding
    enough to make me kind
So I may judge all people
    with my heart and not my mind...
And teach me to be patient
    in everything I do,
Content to trust Your wisdom
    and to follow after You...
And help me when I falter
    and hear me when I pray
And receive me in *Thy Kingdom*
    to dwell with Thee some day.

141

What can be said in conclusion about the essence of Mrs. Rice's life and Mrs. Rice's message? Unlike some writers, hers was one and the same. What she wrote, she believed; what she preached, she practiced. And, if I understood her correctly, her philosophy of giving could be summed up like this:

You Can't Out-give God

When you trust God completely,
  and let Him hold sway,
Your life He will bless,
  every step of the way,
For try as you will
  —it just can't be done—
You will never out-give
  God's only Son.

If you hand God your worries
  He will give you peace,
Spend yourself poor,
  Your wealth He'll increase,
Serve Him as slave,
  He will make you free,
For Him, lose your life
  —find eternity.

If you give Him your troubles,
  His grace will relieve,
Give Him your doubts,
  His power you'll receive,

Give Him your grief,
　　He will dry every tear,
Give Him your weakness,
　　His strength will appear.

If you give Him your hurts,
　　His mercy He'll dole;
Give Him your sins,
　　He will cleanse your soul,
Give Him your heart
　　with no strings attached,
He will fill you with love
　　and joy that's unmatched.

Trust God completely,
　　and let Him hold sway,
Your life He will bless
　　every step of the way,
For try as you will
　　—it just can't be done—
You will never out-give
　　God's only Son.

—FB

143

A Note from Guideposts...

This book was selected for you by the same editorial staff that creates *Guideposts*, a monthly magazine filled with true stories of people's adventures in faith.

If you have found enjoyment in THE PRICELESS GIFT, we think you'll find monthly enjoyment—and inspiration—in the exciting and faith-filled stories that appear in our magazine.

Guideposts is not sold on the newsstand. It's available by subscription only. And subscribing is easy. All you have to do is write Guideposts Associates, Inc.; Carmel, New York 10512. A year's subscription costs only $5.95 in the United States, $7.95 in Canada and overseas.

When you subscribe, each month you can count on receiving exciting new evidence of God's presence, His guidance, and His limitless love for all of us.